The Splendor of France

THE SPLENDOR

Great Châteaux, Mansions, and Country Houses

Photographs by Roberto Schezen
Text by Laure Murat
Introduction by Olivier Bernier
Design by Massimo Vignelli

OF FRANCE

Universe

To Liliane, with all my affection
                    —L.M.

Published in the United States of America in 1995 by
Universe Publishing
A division of Rizzoli International Publications, Inc.
300 Park Avenue South, New York, NY 10010

Clothbound edition first published in the United States of America in 1991 by
Rizzoli International Publications, Inc.

Library of Congress catalog card number 95-060816

Pages 2–3: Façade, La Motte-Glain.
Pages 4–5: Gardens, Villandry.
Pages 6–7: Interior, Hôtel des Ambassadeurs de Hollande.
Page 14: Façade, Château d'O.

Design by Massimo Vignelli

Map by Lundquist Design, New York

Set in type by Graphic Arts Composition, Philadelphia, Pennsylvania

Printed in Italy

Contents

Introduction

Olivier Bernier

Mankind, as everyone knew around the year 1100, was neatly divided into three categories. The clerics who represented God came first, but they were relatively few in number. The peasants and other workers came last, and they made up almost the whole population. Neither group, however, was intended by God to rule the earth: that was reserved for the warriors, whose task was to defend clergy and commonalty alike.

One could always recognize a warrior—or a noble, it was the same thing in those days—because he bore arms and rode a horse; one always knew a nobleman's residence because it was a castle, a fortified place. Soon, as if to clarify it all, castles like Roquetaillade had towered, crenelated ramparts organized around a great central tower which was higher than any other building, except, possibly, the church steeple. There was really no mistaking it: the need for defense had made status visible.

Of course, there were other ways one could recognize a castle: it had walls enclosing the courtyards where the peasants took refuge during times of war; somewhere nearby it had a mill to grind wheat into flour and an oven to bake bread—both these essential technologies were reserved for the nobility as part of many privileges they enjoyed. Even so, castles, inside at least, tended to be dank, dreary places.

With the onset of the Crusades, the French nobles discovered that, in other parts of the world, there were people who lived, not just comfortably, but splendidly. A castle was a fortress, and an emblem of its owner's superior status, but now the nobles realized that it could also be beautiful. By the fourteenth century, the white, multitowered castles shone like jewels; and inside, there were tapestries, silk hangings, and splendidly carved furniture. On the tables, objects made of gold, silver, and precious stones stood near richly illuminated manuscripts, while the lord and lady were dressed in fashions that were as spectacular as they were costly: the castle had become a palace.

Still, it remained a fortress: that was true even of the Louvre, the king's new residence in Paris. But then in the sixteenth century the monarch asserted himself; the internecine wars ended and the French went to Italy. When they brought the Renaissance back with them, the modern château was born.

Because they were no longer planned for defense, these new castles could be designed to give their owners as pleasant a life as possible: they had wide windows to let in the sunlight; and since a good life implied parties, there had to be rooms large enough for dancing, and rooms in which to receive one's friends. A gallery was also essential so that one could still exercise during the winter or in bad weather. A gallery also provided more room to display a wide variety of treasures. And best of all, one no longer had to house a garrison: all the château's interior spaces could be given over to pleasure.

Medieval fortresses had tiny enclosed gardens. Renaissance castles were surrounded by parks. Along with Leonardo da Vinci and a vast quantity of antique sculpture, King François I brought back new ideas for gardens when he returned from Italy in 1515. There were to be views, fountains, and marble or bronze figures, together with carefully pruned bushes and shrubs enclosing parterres of rare flowers, such as the examples we still see today at Villandry. The outdoors, in fact, were becoming an extension of the interiors.

Just as important, a whole new category of people were beginning to own castles: no longer noble, they were simply very rich, and often they became legally noble because they served in the king's courts or loaned money to his treasury. This in itself was a revolution: just sixty years earlier, the enormously wealthy financier Jacques Coeur had not dared do more than build himself a vast and splendid town house. By the year 1500, non-noble castles were sprouting up along the banks of the Loire—then the most fashionable area in France: Villandry and Chenonceau testify to that. Begun in 1513, Chenonceau also set another precedent. Because Thomas Bohier, who helped run the royal treasury, did not hesitate to have the most elegant of castles designed for himself there, François I, after his death, traded the château in exchange for Bohier's debt to the state. Thus a commoner had owned a château worthy of a king.

Although Chenonceau was the last word in elegance, it was still not quite grand enough for a monarch—or his mistress: Henry II, in 1547, gave Chenonceau to the woman he loved, the famously beautiful (and greedy) Diane de Poitiers who promptly added the wing that crosses the river and went on to build herself a vast and superb castle at Anet. A little over a century later, when Louis XIV visited the newly finished château of another financier, François Fouquet, what he saw was the most magnificent building in France, and it took all the glories of Versailles eventually to push Vaux-le-Vicomte back to second place.

In one respect, however, Vaux remains firmly in the first rank: it created a whole new style of architecture, of décor, of living. It was at Vaux that great French classical style was born: Le Vau, its architect, and Le Brun, who painted the ceilings and designed the interiors, were promptly hired by the king, along with Le Nôtre, who was responsible for Vaux's gardens. Together the three men created Versailles, which, in turn, was imitated from Naples to Saint Petersburg.

In many ways, Vaux was the culmination of a long evolution. Here, at last, was the perfect château: large and imposing, but not huge; set among vast gardens where basins, fountains, cascades, and acres of flowers delighted the eye; splendid inside, but still livable. Wood paneling, colorful carpets, painted ceilings, and carved and gilt furniture, all made for the most splendid of environments; but the rooms were of reasonable size. It was possible to live at Vaux with the utmost magnificence, but also to relax and enjoy the country. From the time of its creation until the end of the eighteenth century, every château built in France followed the principles applied at Vaux.

It is this combination of grandeur and a civilized atmosphere that is so characteristic of the French château from the Renaissance onward. Across the Channel, the English aristocracy also commissioned vast and magnificent houses, but they were meant more for sport and display than for conversation, and they were often crushingly grand. The French knew better: together with the art of castle building, they were developing that of conversation; and just because one was in the country did not mean one had to give up the pleasures of the city.

Thus the salon—both the room and the institution—was developed. When, in the 1750s, the Maréchal-duc de Luxembourg retired to his château at Montmorency for three weeks or so, he expected the very best in intellectual atmosphere and got it by frequently inviting Jean-Jacques Rousseau for dinner. Luxembourg himself belonged to the oldest and most illustrious noble family in France, but, even if he spent most of his time at court, he knew that a salon, no matter how handsome, was only meant to serve as the décor for the very best of talk and, of course, music.

That he should only have spent three weeks at Montmorency was also typical

of the way many châteaux were used. Unlike their English counterparts who normally resided nine months of the year on their estates and three in London, the great French aristocrats spent most of their life at court, only rarely leaving for their own country houses. Sometimes the castle in question was conveniently close: the Duke of Luynes could easily spend the occasional day at Dampierre because it was only about an hour's carriage ride from Versailles. Sometimes, as was the case with Josselin, the castle was the hereditary seat of a great dynasty, such as the ducal Rohan family; because it was all the way off in Brittany, Josselin was never visited, and indeed, for a while, turned into a manufacture (it has since been restored by the family).

Still, the political map of Europe sometimes helped. Haroué, just a few miles outside Nancy, was built for the Prince of Beauvau-Craon in 1720 when Lorraine was still a small independent state: thus the prince could pay assiduous court to his sovereign, the Duke of Lorraine, while frequently visiting his own house. Forty-six years later, when Lorraine became a part of France, Haroué suddenly grew far less convenient and was seldom visited. And, of course, there were provincial families who never quite made it to court, simply staying put in their castles.

Still, all these houses had much in common. If they were built or rebuilt after 1650, their architecture was marked by the classic tradition inherited from Le Vau: the interiors might be thoroughly rococo, but the façades are invariably poised, restrained, and elegant. And just as invariably, the ground floor would include an enfilade of a library, several salons (otherwise one might actually be forced into the company of one's spouse) and, from the mid-eighteenth century on, that new specialty, a dining room.

France, in the last fifty years of the Ancien Régime, enjoyed enormous prosperity, and so many castles were built during that time. A number are, of course, near Paris: it was, after all, considered to be the center of the universe and the fount of fashion; but, to a surprising degree, even the distant provinces participated in this building boom. From the 1760s on, as the attraction of the court began to fade, noble families remembered their roots, looked again at their estates, and began to build on them: that was the case, for instance, of the Marquis de La Tour du Pin at Le Bouilh.

As for the owners, they might be almost anyone: a local but prosperous noble family, as at Cheverny; a once-bourgeois family risen to the first rank of the nobility, as at Bizy, whose owner, the Duke of Belle-Isle was the grandson of Fouquet; a member of the high administrative class, as at Saint-Aubin; a *grand seigneur*, such as the Duke of Brissac at the château that bears his name; or simply a rich man.

In fact, by the end of the eighteenth century class distinctions were beginning to fade: while a duke was incomparably grander than a financier or a member of the *Parlement* (which was a court of justice, not a legislature), he was not at all unlikely to marry the daughter of a rich commoner. Today, Champlatreux is a perfect case in point. Built in 1757 for François-Mathieu Molé, heir to one of the most august legal families in France, it passed some hundred years later to the Noailles, one of the grandest names of the old aristocracy, and it still belongs to them today.

That an aristocratic family still resides in a château in present-day France, in turn, calls for a good look at a piece of mythology. The French Revolution, while it eventually ended the monarchy, began by cancelling all the privileges of the aristocracy. Already in the summer and fall of 1789, peasants were rising against their noble landlords and, in some cases, burning down their castles, those symbols of feudal oppression. Then, in 1793, the guillotine got busy, and it is often assumed that most French nobles lost their lives together with their property. As this book shows clearly, the destruction was very far from universal. All through France, castles have happily survived; a few now belong to the French state or to a local government, but most are still in private hands, still lived in, still enjoyed—and far fewer are open to the public than in Great Britain.

Obviously, that seems like a paradox: Great Britain is still a monarchy, France is a republic. Great Britain has had no major political upheaval since the 1640s, France has had several revolutions and several governments that were intent on ending the power of the aristocracy once and for all. That so many old French families should still own their châteaux, however, says something about the permanence of their culture. Of course, the owners have become entitled to state subsidies to carry out repairs; more castles are opening their gates, at least in part, to the public, while others are becoming hotels; but, even then, these great edifices remain what they have always been: unmistakably different from a mere house and proudly distinct; they are still the most visible emblem of privilege and that is lucky for the rest of us For it is in the châteaux so liberally scattered throughout France that some of the best achievements of a dazzling culture have endured for our ever-renewed pleasure.

Location Map

1. Haroué
2. Le Fayel
3. Corbeil-Cerf
4. Bagatelle
5. Balleroy
6. La Bourbansais
7. Rosanbo
8. La Lorie
9. Serrant
10. Brissac
11. Montgeoffroy
12. Le Lude
13. Chenonceau
14. Vaux-le-Vicomte
15. Courances
16. Dampierre
17. Groussay
18. Anet
19. Hôtel des Ambassadeurs de Hollande
20. Hôtel Lambert
21. Tanlay
22. Cormatin
23. Moncley
24. Ainay-le-Vieil
25. Ansouis
26. Barbentane
27. Roquetaillade
28. Château-Lafite

NORTH SEA

ENGLAND

BELGIUM

GERMANY

English Channel

Lille

PICARDY

4

LUX.

Le Havre

Rouen

3

2

ÎLE DE FRANCE

5

LORRAINE

NORMANDY

Seine

Marne

Strasbourg

7

18

Paris

19–20

6

17

16

14

ALSACE

BRITTANY

MAINE

15

CHAMPAGNE

1

Rennes

21

8

FRANCHE-COMTÉ

12

Nantes

11

Loire

Dijon

22

9

10

13

SWITZERLAND

ANJOU

BERRY

BURGUNDY

F R A N C E

24

POITOU

Clermont-Ferrand

23

Atlantic Ocean

LIMOUSIN

Lyons

SAVOY

LYONNAIS

28

ITALY

Bordeaux

Dordogne

DAUPHINE

27

Rhône

AQUITAINE

26

25

Toulouse

PROVENCE

GASCONY

LANGUEDOC

Marseille

S P A I N

Mediterranean

Haroué, Lorraine

"Even though this building is modern, it was built up around the old towers of an ancient château that, being in a state of decay, could no longer exist," wrote Germain Boffrand, the architect of Haroué and author of *Livre d'architecture, contenant les principes généraux de cet art* (Book of architecture, containing the general principles of this art) that appeared in 1745. In 1753, however, the second edition of this same book did not mention the plans nor did it make note of Haroué. This surprising decision, which history soon repaired, was Boffrand's unjust attempt to minimize his accomplishments at Haroué.

Starting with the sixteenth-century decaying house-fortress of the Bassompierre family, Boffrand, one of the top architects of France, built the new dwelling between 1721 and 1729 for the Marquis Marc de Beauvau, a powerful gentleman of Lorraine and a future viceroy of Tuscany. The horseshoe-shaped plan, the moats, and the corner towers were preserved, but the château itself was completely remodeled. The colonnades, cornices, and porticoes gave the new building a princely appearance.

Haroué, a dwelling of "Parisian" elegance, retained its regional identity: Boffrand surrounded himself with the best artists of Lorraine such as the sculptor Barthélémy Guibal, who realized the group of putti surrounding the château, and Jean Lamour, creator of the famous grillwork at the Place Stanislas in Nancy, who executed the ironwork at Haroué, notably the graceful handrail of the main staircase.

A model of classical architecture, Haroué displays one of the best-preserved interior décors: the salon furniture by Bellangé that comes from the château at Saint-Ouen, the family portraits, and the state room enlivened by Italianate furniture, all contribute equally to make Haroué a château where history and the art of living are in harmony.

Above and opposite: *The English-style garden is punctuated by statues whose expressions are often enigmatic.*

Above: *The entrance is evocative of Boffrand's work with de Cotte and Hardouin-Mansart on the Place Vendôme.*

Opposite: *Detail, tapestry illustrating a scene from the history of Alexander the Great on display in Haroué.*

Opposite: *The château's salon is dedicated to King Louis XVIII. In the painting by Gérard, the monarch is portrayed seated at his writing desk. The elegant furnishings in the room, signed by the renowned Bellangé, were owned by the king.*

Above: *The dining room of Haroué, often bathed in a soft light, is distinctive for its decorative simplicity.*

Above: *Mid-eighteenth-century painted walls are the highlight of the tower sitting room overlooking the garden.*

Opposite: *King Stanislas Leszcynski was one of the famous guests who stayed in this elaborately furnished bedroom.*

Le Fayel, Picardy

Opposite: *Jacques Bruant began building the Château Le Fayel around 1650. Work was completed six years later.*

Begun around 1650, Le Fayel stands without ostentation or sentimentality before a mirror of water that reflects its image. Jacques Bruant, whose brother, Libéral Bruant, became famous in the seventeenth century when he constructed the Hôtel des Invalides and the Hôpital de la Salpétrière in Paris, made the plans for the château. It is thought that the architect finished work in 1656—the year when Louis XIV received with great pomp Queen Christine of Sweden who came to stay in France.

If the exterior evokes the seventeenth century, it is the Empire style that was chosen for the interior décor: stools, armchairs, patterned rugs, and silks are in the style of the Napoleonic era.

Opposite: *In the salons of Le Fayel, the taste for the Empire style reigns.* Above: *A bust keeps watch over the premises.*

Above: *The royal bee motif appears on the carpet in this salon filled with mahogany and gilded bronze furnishings.*

Opposite: *The unique circular bookshelves at Le Fayel house many precious and historic volumes and manuscripts.*

Corbeil-Cerf, Picardy

Opposite and overleaf: *The gardens, conceived by the Marquis de Lubersac during the late nineteenth century, frame the château with two façades, one of which dates back to the Renaissance and the other to the period of the reign of Henry IV.*

Hidden and protected behind a promenade of linden trees linked by ivy garlands is a château of modest size. Plant boxes hold lively flowers and plants, and a rose garden frames the château; a park, punctuated by hedgerows with niches for statues, unfolds behind the façade. Conceived at the end of the nineteenth century by the Marquis de Lubersac, this clever landscape gives Corbeil-Cerf its charm.

Two roofs of unequal height cover the main part of the building, whose two façades were erected in the Renaissance and during the reign of Henry IV respectively. Also from this period, 1595 to be precise, is the contiguous house on the east side of the property, with its remarkable décor of sculpted fruits and draperies.

At one time expanded to include a twisting wing—which was destroyed in the nineteenth century—the château has not left the name of its builder but only of its owner around 1620, Charles de Brinon, an ordinary gentleman from the Chambers of the King; he was buried at Saint-Severin and his heart was sent to Corbeil-Cerf. Such loyalty to a place was passed down through the centuries, which is what happened when the family of Pierre de Lubersac inherited Corbeil-Cerf in 1769. After this time the interior décor of this admirably well maintained château was embellished with precious and unique objects, ranging from small eighteenth-century boxes to a collection of old books, not to mention the paintings of our modern masters.

Opposite: *The central salon combines the refined style of the eighteenth century with the comfort of English interiors.*

Above: *The charm of Corbeil-Cerf rests in the precision of its interior design: each object plays a role in the décor.*

Opposite: *The original latticework on the walls provides a visual link between the dining room and the gardens.*

Above: *In the park, the statues, niched in bowers, are from the Château de Rocquencourt near Versailles.*

Bagatelle, Picardy

Opposite: *Bagatelle was heightened by a story in 1763; two wings were added at the beginning of the twentieth century.*

Derived from the Latin, "bagatelle," or "tower of the juggler," generally evokes something of little importance, frivolous and light like a passing fancy. Architecture took up this term to designate a folly, a building type very much in vogue in the eighteenth century, such as the one that the Count of Artois built for Marie-Antoinette on the outskirts of Paris: namely, the small château of Bagatelle.

The pavilion that the clothier Abraham Van Robais undertook between 1751 and 1754 in the community of Abbeville near Amiens also bears this name— Bagatelle. From the beginning, the modest *maison des champs* (country house), comprising a simple ground floor and three rooms, was a place for business meetings where the owner's profession is alluded to by the ornamentation of the façades on which sculpted pieces of fabric are interwoven.

Starting in 1763, Bagatelle was expanded and an attic-style second floor was added; just before the Revolution a mansard roof replaced the terrace in Trianon style. A charming and outstanding example of a brick-and-stone château, Bagatelle has left the name of its architect a mystery, though the name of Jacques-François Blondel has recently been proposed. It was not until the twentieth century that Bagatelle attained its present form. At this time Paul de Wailly, the new owner, called upon the architect Parent to expand his estate: two wings, each one ending with a pavilion, finally "completed" this dwelling without altering its order or its harmony.

Opposite: *The delicate ironwork is testimony to the talent of the Abbeville workers in the eighteenth century.*

Above and overleaf: *Bagatelle retains its original décor, most notably in the central summer salon.*

Balleroy, Normandy

It was for Jean II Choisy, councilor of state and later chancellor of Gaston of Orléans, that François Mansart drew up the plans in 1626 for the château of Balleroy, thus executing one of his very first works. The large scope of his project called for the reconstruction of the entire town so that the surrounding landscape would regain its balance. Ten years later, the central body of the building, the two corner pavilions in the main courtyard, and the outbuildings were finished, constituting one of the most felicitous symbols of the Louis XIII style.

The building owes its dynamism to the mixture of shale and stones from Caen that underlies the structure of the château, but it is the pyramidal configuration ending with the chimneys, the central skylight, and the concentric staircase rising from the foot of the entrance terrace that enhance its eloquence and grandeur.

In the interior, the décors executed during the Grand Siècle have been preserved: the energetic ceiling moldings, the woodcarvings, and above all the paintings by Pierre Mignard (1612–1695) in the salon of portraits of the House of France—over the fireplace Louis XIII assumes the principal role, while Apollo, preceded by Aurora, decorates the oval of the ceiling. Nothing has altered this arrangement over the centuries: the nineteenth century was content to add only a few boxwood decorations in the French style in the first two courts . . . thus making Balleroy, for many of its visitors, the very emblem of the French château.

Opposite: *On display in the grand salon is a series of royal portraits, including one of Louis XIII above the fireplace.*

Above: *Aurora scatters garlands of flowers on the oval ceiling painted by Pierre Mignard (1612–1695).*

La Bourbansais, Brittany

Of its Gallo-Roman origins, La Bourbansais has retained a marshy terrain and its inherited name, *Terre des Bourbans* (Land of the Bourbans). But we need to go back to 1583 to find the history of its construction, commissioned as it was by the du Breil family. At this time Brittany, only recently reunited with France, was at peace: the architecture of pleasure soon succeeded the architecture of war. Was it in celebration of the end of hostilities that the owners topped their towers with baroque roofs surmounted with campaniles? La Bourbansais still remains a typical example of the regional taste of this period as it adapted to a new way of life.

To relieve the humidity, the ground floor of La Bourbansais was raised to constitute a false floor, the first having been reserved for reception rooms. Work continued in the seventeenth century, with the alterations of two buildings on the west side, one of which housed a chapel later transferred to the north. With the eighteenth century came a softening of the château's still-defensive aspect, and a strengthening of its apparent symmetry: the portal and the moats underwent alterations as did the southern façade, with two lateral small pavilions and their framework *à la Mansart*.

Though it risked being razed and replaced by grand projects in the nineteenth and twentieth centuries, La Bourbansais somehow resisted, appearing today almost exactly as it was at the moment of its construction.

Rosanbo, Brittany

As its etymology indicates, Rosanbo (or Rock on the Bô, the name of the little stream nearby) is a building as strong and impassive as the stone of Brittany.

The old fortress, which reached its present configuration in the sixteenth century, reveals from its entrance a massive porch and pavilions. Reinforced by powerful buttresses, Rosanbo took on a more graceful appearance at the end of the seventeenth century, when it was altered according to the taste of the new owner, Louis Le Pelletier, son of the comptroller of finances under Louis XIV and first president of the parliament of Paris. This château came into the hands of a *noblesse de robe* family, and the general appearance of the château took on a deliberately classical turn to compensate for its lack of symmetry: the entrance buildings are embellished by mansard roofs and the windows are harmonized in the "French style." According to the wishes of the owner, the enclosure—as the parks in Brittany are called—is inspired by the gardens of Versailles: the border of parterres bears testimony to this, as do the stone pool framing a mirror of water in front of the château and the rigorously maintained pathways whose trees form a vault designed to increase the pleasure of a promenade.

Restored in the nineteenth century after several decades of neglect, Rosanbo has today recovered its splendor. The "white lady" who, according to a persistent legend, has haunted the château at night, could certainly attest to that.

Opposite: *A more classical character is evident in the details of the seventeenth-century façade of the château.*

Above: *The trees lining the garden walk form a natural vault, adding a sense of mystery to the place.*

Above: *A view of a pleasant landscape is depicted in the large tapestry on display in the library at Rosanbo.*

Opposite: *The library has an atmosphere that encourages study. The tapestry's position gives the impression of a window view.*

La Lorie, Loire Region

Begun in the seventeenth century for René Le Pelletier, grand provost of Anjou, La Lorie was greatly expanded in the following century: from gentleman's quarters to château. Charles Constantin, the new owner, had only to take one bold step. The enlarged building with wings and outbuildings at right angles was embellished by a marble salon and a chapel. But the ambitious Charles Constantin did not stop there: at the end of the eighteenth century he installed one of the first stud farms of the region on his property, thus making La Lorie renowned in Anjou. The Revolution would put an end to these prodigalities and the buildings suffered from various occupations.

Enthusiasm returned in the nineteenth century. During this period the gallery of the ground floor was altered, impressing its magnificence on the whole. The majestic rhythm of the vestibule that leads to the main staircase is marked by the Tuscan-style columns and pilasters that support it, as well as by the blue-and-white vases and porcelains dispersed at regular intervals in niches.

Gardens transformed into the French style in 1867 frame this estate that would no longer have to suffer the injuries of time.

Above: *Detail, one of many sculptures inhabiting the restored French gardens on the grounds of the château.*

Opposite: *The handsome southern façade of the château overlooks gardens restored in the early twentieth century.*

Opposite: *The light-filled grand marble salon was decorated by Italian craftsmen in the late eighteenth century.*

Above: *The Louis XVI armchairs are upholstered in velvet from Genoa and are stamped Pluvinet.*

Above and opposite: *The Tuscan-columned entrance hall was redecorated during the nineteenth century.*

Serrant, Loire Region

On the road from Angers to Nantes stands Serrant, proudly anchored inside its moats. A majestic Renaissance construction, this château was begun in 1546 by Philibert de l'Orme for Charles de Brie on the site of an old fortress. The central building, the staircase, entrance stairs, the dovecote, and the stables also date back to this time. Under the aegis of its new owner, Guillaume Bautru, a court jester, academician, and diplomatic agent for Richelieu, work was taken up again in the seventeenth century. The master of the house, who, according to his son, "cared very little for his chapel and very much for his cuisine and library," took up the construction of the two wings and the south tower before his death in 1655. Twenty years later, Jules Hardouin-Mansart built a chapel here for the Marquis de Vaubrun, which soon after was joined by the mausoleum of Coysevox; in the eighteenth century, the château was finished and the park altered to the English style by the Walshes, a family of Irish origin who bought Serrant in 1749. In the nineteenth century some late restorations were made by the architect Lucien Magne, who added a balustrade and topped the windows with cornices. It is unusual that the successive retouchings of Serrant did not alter it in any way: the château has kept the unity of its Renaissance plan and its martial bearing, as well as its admirably preserved interior décor. Spared from the ravages of wars and of time, Serrant could represent the "rock" of which French poet Stéphane Mallarmé speaks "which imposed a milestone on the infinite."

Opposite: *In the chapel, Corinthian columns frame a monument to Marquis de Vaubrun made by Antoine Coysevox.*

Above: *The monument's gilded bas-relief frieze depicts the battle of Altenheim during which the marquis met his death.*

Above: *Above the library fireplace, the large painting records the meeting in Scotland of Prince Charles-Edouard Stuart of the French royal court and Antoine Walsh, one of the members of the family that originally owned the Serrant estate.*

Opposite: *The library of Serrant, the largest room in the château, contains more than ten thousand volumes.*

Above and opposite: *Seventeenth-century tapestries hang on the walls of the comfortably furnished grand salon.*

Above: *A bust of the empress Marie-Louise by Canova surveys the bedroom designed for Josephine and Napoleon I.*

Opposite: *The swan, an emblem of Josephine and the lords of Serrant, is found on chair arms and the bed frame.*

Above and opposite: *In the bedroom of the mistress of the house is a Gobelins tapestry featuring a Chinese scene.*

Brissac, Loire Region

The whimsical eclecticism of Brissac's façades can be disconcerting at first glance. Begun at the end of the Middle Ages, taken up and then abandoned at the beginning of the seventeenth century, it is, according to its owner, "a new château half-built within an old, partially destroyed château."

The history of "France's first skyscraper" goes back to 1455, when the two towers of the Levant façade, with machicolations in profile, were built side by side. Brissac then belonged to Pierre de Brézé, minister under Charles VII, and its appearance is similar to those châteaux of the region, such as Langeais or Plessis-Bourré. But it was Jacques Corbineau, architect of Port-Louis, the citadel at Lorient, who was actually responsible for the *toute en hauteur* (completely vertical) configuration of the new home of the Cossé family, counts of Brissac. As early as 1606 work was undertaken on the base of the first château that suffered terribly from wars and invasions: in the forty-three-meter-high keep, one single dwelling space—as opposed to the two foreseen at the beginning of the project—was erected. In the north, a rectangular pavilion seven stories high was added while the so-called De Bonnivet terrace took shape in the southwest. The project, undoubtedly judged to be too grandiose, was halted in 1621. The king and the court would nevertheless come and stroll here in the following centuries, until the Revolution temporarily interrupted the rhythm of parties given here. Continually restored and maintained from the nineteenth century to the present (the private theater, for example, has recently been repaired), Brissac has never lost its uniqueness.

Opposite: *Brissac's two towers are the only remnants of the original castle built during the fifteenth century.*

Above: *The coat of arms of Cossé-Brissac, cut in bedrock from the Loire, welcomes the visitor in the vestibule.*

Above: *Sculpted, painted, and enhanced with gold, the ceilings of Brissac are an important facet of its décor.*

Opposite: *In the grand salon, a Gobelins tapestry, signed and dated Audran, 1782, depicts Don Quixote's adventures.*

Opposite: *The reconciliation between Marie de Médicis and her son, Louis XIII, took place in this salon in 1620.*

Above and overleaf: *Rich tapestries, haute-époque furniture, and beautiful ceilings are seen throughout the rooms.*

Montgeoffroy, Loire Region

Opposite: *Montgeoffroy, designed by the architect Barré, stands regally above a field of bright sunflowers.*

An illustrious family fief, Montgeoffroy represents the ideal dwelling of a gentleman of the Ancien Régime. With its silhouette standing out against a field of sunflowers, its décor in pastel tints, and its salons with open doors through which light streams, the château could have been a theater for the most charming of Marivaux's plays. Such is the impression one gets upon entering this well-preserved place that rises behind grillwork done in the Louis XV style and signed by Mistouflet.

Begun in 1773 according to the plans of Nicolas Barré, architect of Le Marais and brilliant inspiriter of the royal square in Brussels, the château was built for the Marshal of Contades. Barré's building has a calm simplicity, and it skillfully integrates the two lateral pavilions and the chapel (1543) that remain from the old château.

In laying out the spaces without pretentiousness, all of which were rectangular except for the oval dining room, Barré favored comfort and convenience: rest, play, conversations, and parties were an integral part of the décor. The furniture, mostly commissioned from the cabinetmakers Garnier, Gourdin, and Durand by the marshal's daughter-in-law, has kept intact its freshness and arrangement in each room . . . so much so that Montgeoffroy, perfectly illustrating the Transition style (Louis XV–Louis XVI), remains the example par excellence of the art of living in eighteenth-century France.

Opposite: *The elegant salons of the grand estate epitomize the art of living during the century of Marivaux.*

Above: *The oval dining room.* Overleaf: *A well-organized display of copper pots hangs on one wall of the château kitchen.*

Le Lude, Loire Region

All that remains today of the thirteenth-century fortress of Le Lude are the stone foundations, anchored in dried-up moats. The imposing château that sits on the banks of the Loire acquired its first appearance in the Renaissance when it was abandoned as a military bastion to become truly a "dwelling of pleasure." This change came about under the aegis of the Daillon, an old noble family from Poitou, seven members of which occupied the château in succession from 1457 to 1685.

The dwelling, after it was reinforced by Jehan de Daillon, underwent some notable transformations in the course of the sixteenth century: the defense towers disappeared between 1520 and 1530; the southern façade that has been attributed to the architect Jean Gendrot, master of works for King René of Anjou, and the main courtyard, both examples of the Renaissance style, tempered the feudal harshness of the château. In the seventeenth century, the gardens were divided into parterres and the terrace was added, crowned by an elegant balustrade along which Madame de Sévigné loved to stroll.

From 1685 to 1751, Le Lude passed from hand to hand, a victim of repeated desertions, before being taken up again by M. du Velaer, a wealthy entrepreneur of Dutch origin who revived the château. His heir, the Marquise de Vieuville, commissioned architect Nicolas Barré, a student of Gabriel, to construct the Louis XVI façade in 1787. This last architectural contribution gave Le Lude the aspect of a château that has permanently opted for the sweetness of living over the rigors of the past.

Opposite: *Behind the eighteenth-century façade, the grand salon is decorated in harmonious red and gold tones.*

Above: *A Flanders tapestry of the seventeenth century hangs on one wall of the spacious dining room.*

Above: *A portrait of General de Talhouët's wife hangs on the wall of this salon at the Château Le Lude.*

Opposite: *In a bedroom decorated in Empire style, a portrait of General de Talhouët and his sister is on display.*

Above: *The Henry IV bedroom, with walls
covered in Cordovan leather, is named in
honor of its most famous guest.*

Above: *A seventeenth-century Beauvais tapestry was used to upholster the furniture in the library.*

Above: *An intricately painted ceiling hangs above the small, Renaissance-style chapel room at Le Lude.*

Opposite: *This small chapel room was plastered over during the Revolution and restored in the twentieth century.*

Chenonceau, Loire Region

The châteaux of the Loire have long had the status of myth. Among them, Chenonceau retains a particular prestige. "The ladies' château," where the most famous love stories of Renaissance France was made and destroyed, has certainly earned its nickname. Built according to the instructions of a woman, Catherine Bohier, it passed into the hands of King François I who appropriated it for his hunts and pleasures, then, at his death, to his son Henry II. Chenonceau was given to Diane de Poitiers, mistress of King Henry II, and she reigned there alone, embellishing it with glorious gardens and a bridge, built by Philibert de l'Orme, which connected the château to the left bank of the Cher.

Catherine de Médicis, widow of Henry II, succeeded Diane de Poitiers as owner of the château. To mark her triumph, the avenged regent organized dazzling receptions in the gallery, erected by Androuet du Cerceau on the arches that span the river.

Having remained in the royal family for a long time, the property became too provincial for a court so close to Versailles and was finally abandoned. It was up to the philosophers of the Enlightenment to take up the torch much later: Voltaire, Montesquieu, Buffon, and Madame du Deffand, among others, shone there in the salon of the new master of the house, Claude Dupin, one of the richest *fermiers généraux* (men who "farmed" certain taxes in France between 1697 and 1789) of the century, and his wife, whose secretary was Jean-Jacques Rousseau. "We had a good time in this beautiful place, ate sumptuously; I became as fat as a monk there. Music was played, and comedy was performed there. I composed a play in verse entitled *L'Allée de Sylvie* (Sylvie's path), the name of a path in the park that borders the Cher," wrote the author of *Emile*, the treatise on education that he began at this time.

Bought in 1864 by another woman, Madame Pelouze, the château was restored and embellished: the gallery had a *fin-de-siècle* décor (unfortunately gone today), and the park regained its charm. It is with the family of Henri Menier, a noted industrialist, that the story of this famous "château-bridge," this spectacular architectural metaphor of the passage from the Middle Ages to the Renaissance, comes to a close.

Vaux-le-Vicomte, Paris Region

Like a challenge thrown at history, Vaux-le-Vicomte was designed and built in five years by three men (Le Vau, Le Brun, Le Nôtre) for the glory of one: Nicolas Fouquet, superintendent of finances under Louis XIV. Three hundred and fifty years later, this masterpiece, having remained intact, does not suffer in comparison to other châteaux of France—except for Versailles with which it had already competed for splendor at the time of its construction. But one did not compete with the Sun King: Fouquet was to learn this at his expense.

The ambitious superintendent, who wanted to build a dwelling worthy of his status, commissioned the greatest artists of his time to fulfill his wishes: Louis Le Vau designed the plans for the château, Andre Le Nôtre those for the garden, and the painter Charles Le Brun designed the interior décor where the Salon of the Muses prevailed. Punctuating the park are statues and grottoes sheltering river gods.

On August 17, 1661, Fouquet gave a famous party in honor of the king and his court in his new estate. And on September 5 he was arrested by d'Artagnan under orders of the monarch. Certainly taken aback by so much ostentation, Louis XIV, with the help of Colbert, comptroller of finances, had been preparing Fouquet's downfall for a long time, suspecting him of misappropriation of funds. In spite of his proven devotion, Fouquet remained, in the eyes of the king, the ambitious one who saw himself as the new "arbiter of State." The arrogant sumptuousness of that last party only confirmed this suspicion and evoked a brutal response to Fouquet's family motto: *Quo non ascendet* (To what heights won't he climb?) As Voltaire later wrote: "The 17th of August, at six o'clock in the evening, Fouquet was the king of France; at two o'clock in the morning, he was nothing." Judged, banished, but not condemned by the judges until after a three-year trial, Fouquet was the object of royal vindictiveness until his death. For the first time in the history of France, the chief of state increased the punishment of the accused: Louis XIV asked for life imprisonment (instead of banishment, which had been recommended by the court) for Fouquet, who ended his days in prison in 1680.

After the arrest of the superintendent, Vaux-le-Vicomte was confiscated from his descendants, not to be restituted to them until twelve years later. Furniture, valuable objects, and tapestries were requisitioned by the crown. Le Vau was put in charge of expanding Versailles, Le Nôtre was asked to re-create the gardens, and Le Brun was named first painter by the king.

Henceforth, Vaux-le-Vicomte could traverse all the other vagaries of history. That is what it did, always with as much arrogance as brilliance.

Opposite: *Le Brun's mastery is easily recognizable in the painted décor of the château's dining room.*

Above: *On the ceiling, the central image,* Peace Bringing Abundance, *alludes to the 1659 Treaty of the Pyrenees.*

Above: *Above the antechamber, framed in stucco, is a scene in monochrome of Diana removing her shoes after the hunt.*

Opposite: *An equestrian portrait of Louis XIV, painted by Houasse, dominates this antechamber at Vaux-le-Vicomte. This spacious room has served as a library since before the Revolution. The desk in the foreground is stamped Levasseur.*

Opposite: *The interior scheme of the king's bedroom anticipates the décor that Le Brun was to achieve at Versailles.*

Above: *On the bedroom ceiling, the allegory of Time lifting Truth to heaven is framed by stuccoes of winged women and helmeted cupids attributed to the artists Legendre and Girardon. Overleaf: A view of the magnificent gardens of Vaux-le-Vicomte.*

Opposite: *The symmetry of the façade of Vaux-le-Vicomte is set off by the gardens.* Above: *A fountain sculpture.*

Above: *In the gardens, originally designed by Le Nôtre, the placement of stone sculptures adds to the refined atmosphere.*

Opposite: *At Vaux-le-Vicomte, the vista is as controlled as every other aspect of the design of the residence and gardens.*

Courances, Paris Region

Opposite and overleaf: *Famous for its gardens, Courances assumed its present form in the early seventeenth century.*

Legend—which is always tempting to believe—has it that Courances acquired its name from the running waters *(eaux courantes)* that traverse its grounds. Inspired by Le Nôtre (1613–1700), then redone by the landscape gardener Achille Duchêne at the beginning of the twentieth century, these gardens are among the most beautiful in France: the constantly changing vistas follow the course of the springs, canals, and cascades, creating solitary islets here and there, like the Anglo-Japanese garden created between the two world wars by the Marquise de Ganay. Swans and statues punctuate the pathway designed to be resplendent in all seasons. A statue of the nymph Arethusa comes from Marly, the residence built for Louis XIV by Jules Hardouin-Mansart.

The château was built at the heart of the green paradise and was probably reconstructed in the sixteenth century by Gilles Le Breton, who collaborated with Pierre Lescot to build Fleury. In the seventeenth century, the château was again greatly revised and finally reached its present form. The architect Hippolyte Destailleurs added some last embellishments in 1870, under the direction of the new master, the Baron de Haber: at this time the entire property was restored (Courances had been abandoned for almost forty years) and the monumental staircase, which is a copy of the one at the palace of Fontainebleau, was installed on the front façade. Thus the royal appearance of Courances was only strengthened with time.

Opposite: *In the gardens, a seventeenth-century sculpture of a bather by Claude Poirier comes from Marly.*

Above: *A sandstone dolphin head is just one of many sculptural treasures found on the Courances property.*

Above: *Stone statues stand along the pathways in the extensive park surrounding the Château de Courances.*

Opposite: *Plants and shrubs from around the world can be viewed in the Anglo-Japanese garden on the grounds.*

Above and opposite: *The peaceful, well-maintained park surrounding Courances offers a variety of hidden treasures.*

Above: *Stone personages and animals animate the estate's grounds.* Opposite: *A vista through the trees.*

Opposite: *Waterways dot the landscape.*
Above: *Swans glide along the grand canal of the property.*

Above: *The château is named for the running waters that can be seen throughout the beautiful landscape.*

Above: *A magnificent ornamental waterway on the grounds at Courances.* Overleaf: *The entrance façade.*

Opposite: *A tree-lined pathway.* Above: *A small sixteenth-century building is found at the end of one path.*

Above: *The enchanting Anglo-Japanese
garden at Courances is a twentieth-century
creation, planned between the world wars.*

Above and overleaf: *The Anglo-Japanese
garden was planned by the Marquise de Ganay
with the help of an English friend.*

Dampierre, Paris Region

Opposite, first and second overleafs: *Dampierre is one of the jewels of the seventeenth century.*

Damna pietra—damned stone—for what dark adventures was Dampierre the setting to merit such an etymology? Witness to the intrigues of the Duchess of Chevreuse, who was called "the most beautiful amazon of the Fronde," the château was reconstructed at the end of the seventeenth century according to plans by Jules Hardouin-Mansart. Le Nôtre designed the gardens where the king and his court would stroll until the Revolution.

During the nineteenth century, Honoré d'Albert de Luynes, scholar and patron who undertook the promotion of "modern art," magisterially transformed part of the interior décor. Ingres, de Luynes's colleague at the Institut de France, endowed Dampierre with a work that was "at once a treasure of art and a lesson in high morals." In 1849, the master, inspired but lazy, left unfinished two monumental compositions in the Room of Minerva that had been designed by the architect Duban: *The Golden Age* and *The Age of Iron*. The polychrome décor, executed by some thirty painters, among them the Flandrin brothers and Paul Delaroche, reinterprets with eloquence images inherited from Pompeii and the Renaissance.

Climbing the stairs of Dampierre also brings back reminiscences: the Grand Siècle appears here, and Hellenism is evoked by the graceful sleeping Penelope in marble by the sculptor Cavelier. Thanks to the discernment of its owners, Dampierre has inherited numerous interiors that today constitute a history book of taste, which the rereadings of time have not altered.

Above and opposite: *On the walls above the Duban-designed staircase are detailed urns painted by Picot.*

Above: *Beautifully detailed stucco figures line the walls of the richly decorated stairway at Château de Dampierre.*

Opposite: *Dampierre's magnificence culminates in the room of Minerva. Sculpted by Simart, the figure of the goddess of war stands in front of the large-scale painting,* The Golden Age, *by the renowned artist Jean Auguste Dominique Ingres.*

Above: *Approximately forty artists, over several years, participated in the decoration of the château's interior.*

Opposite: *Framed by two caryatides, a seventeenth-century bronze delicately turns its back to the garden view.*

Groussay, Paris Region

Opposite: *Carlos de Beistegui, with the help of Emilio Terry, added two arched wings to the Empire façade.*

In restoring Groussay, its owner, Carlos de Beistegui (1894–1970), seems to have followed a "playful step-by-step reforming of rituals" of which Jean Cocteau speaks in one of his poems. In any case, it is with a festive air that this amateur, unaware of prejudices, transformed a nineteenth-century building into an extravagant home: it is here that Louis XIII finds himself next to Napoleon, and Henry II meets Marie-Antoinette under the amused gazes of a neoclassical bust. But simply to unite different styles in this house would have been too easy and undoubtedly erroneous. In order to achieve the proper harmony, it was necessary to reinterpret, even to reinvent earlier styles in order to create a unique taste: the "Beistegui taste," which a number of decorators would set about imitating with varying degrees of success. Henceforth, it would be acceptable to combine blue with green, floral motifs with checkerboards, the English nineteenth-century style with that of the Haute Époque.

At Groussay, this idea of décor, always nurtured by erudite sources, surely went side by side with a sense of play, which gives the place coherence. Thus, in a variety of styles, Carlos de Beistegui gave "play" different definitions. The library, for example, uses illusion (trompe l'oeil effects on the ceiling and the walls, convex mirrors, and so on) to temper the grandiose proportions (its height corresponds to that of the château, rising from the ground floor to the third floor). The garden offers a diversion rhymed in stages, from the Tempietto to the column of Trajan, passing the Palladian bridge. Of course, balls took place in the salons of Groussay where the grand gentry of the area came to celebrate after World War II. The ultimate variation on play was embodied in the theater, installed in one of the extreme ends of the château: for its inauguration Marcel Achard wrote *The Impromptu of Groussay* that put friends of the host on stage, played by actors of the Comédie Française. "Life imitates art," Oscar Wilde used to say. Thanks to Carlos de Beistegui, Groussay would be one of the most eloquent proofs of this motto and of its significance.

Above and opposite: *Interiors by Carlos de Beistegui are as much a surprise as the painted metal tent in the garden.*

Above and opposite: *A rich array of buildings dot the grounds, from a Palladian bridge to a brick pyramid.*

Above and opposite: *Follies, such as a Chinese pagoda and a viewing column, enrich the eccentric landscape.*

Above: *The symmetry of the mahogany-covered double-flight staircase is echoed in the decoration of the hall.*

Opposite: *As one passes through the succession of salons at Groussay, an astonishing variety of interior effects is achieved. In this stunning salon, the same sumptuous fabric as the one selected by the queen for the Versailles palace adorns the walls.*

Opposite: *The library is Groussay's most spectacular room. Despite the numerous objects, symmetry is achieved.*

Above: *In the Dutch salon, furnishings in a range of styles are combined within a color scheme of blues and greens.*

Opposite: *Curved banquettes line one of the two dramatic and colorful semicircular hallways inside the house.*

Above: *One curved hallway leads to a private theater, rare in French residences, decorated in brilliant reds and blues.*

Anet, Paris Region

Of the stone souvenirs left by Philibert de l'Orme (c. 1510–c. 1570), Anet is undoubtedly one of the most arresting. Though the hazards of time have sadly tested this château (of the three original wings, only one, partially reconstructed, survives), its former majesty can still be felt in the chapel (1550) and the portal (1552). The architect began assimilating the current models of Italian and French architecture. This was done for the illustrious Diane de Poitiers, the mistress of King Henry II. A joining of love and power was symbolically celebrated in the château with intertwining monograms: the H for Henry and lunar crescent of Diane. Anet was ostentatious then: the entire court came to dance on the tiles created by the ceramicist Macéo Abaquesne and to admire the collections of Saint-Porchaire, Venetian glass, books (171 manuscripts on vellum, dispersed in the eighteenth century), and stained-glass windows in grisaille attributed to Jean Goujon. At the death of the sovereign in 1559, Anet became the retreat of Diane, who had fallen in disgrace under the reign of Catherine de Médicis. Seven years later, the "Dame d'Anet" passed away in turn. Her son-in-law, Claude de Lorraine, Duke of Aumâle, raised a memorial chapel in her name where her body was transported in 1576.

Energetically taken up again in the nineteenth century after many mutilations, abandonments, and other ravages, the château slowly recovered its soul, becoming once again "the charming residence/that glen where Nature/Exhausts its treasures/To please Love . . ." (Chevalier de Florian).

Opposite: *Only one of the three original Renaissance-period wings at Anet has survived the centuries.*

Above: *The Duke of Vendôme initiated the restoration of the château. This monumental staircase leads to the ballroom. The stark clarity of the light underlines the refinement of the forged-iron banister bearing the insignia of the duke.*

Above: *The crescent moon, the symbol of Diane de Poitiers, is intertwined with the monogram and royal crown insignia of her lover, King Henry II of France, on the wood-paneled library ceiling and in many places throughout the château.*

Opposite: *Carved wood paneling còvers every surface of the comfortable library of the Château d'Anet.*

Opposite: *Sixteenth-century d'Aubusson tapestries depicting the hunt hang on either side of the dining salon fireplace.*

Above: *In the nineteenth century, the vaulted ceilings above this salon were restored to their original grandeur.*

Above: *In a sleeping chamber, Diane de Poitiers's coat of arms is depicted on the wall between circa 1552 tapestries.*

Opposite: *The regal bed of Diane de Poitiers is displayed in this splendidly decorated sleeping chamber at the château.*

Above: *Adjacent to Diane's sleeping chamber, the dressing room features a magnificent stained-glass window.*

Opposite: *The chapel, designed by Philibert de l'Orme in the form of a Greek cross, was built in 1550.*

Opposite: *Trompe l'oeil details, attributed to Jean Goujon, enhance the interior effect of the chapel at Anet.*

Above: *The chapel dome was one of the first built in France. Its decoration mirrors the tilework of the floor.*

Above and opposite: *The monument representing Diane de Poitiers in prayer is probably the work of Pierre Bontemps.*

Hôtel des Ambassadeurs de Hollande, Paris

"I don't have much praise for the actual building (of this house), but the wonderful layout and magnificence of the work, the beautiful paintings and sculptures made by the excellent Masters of Paris, the entrance door, the Chapel, and the staircase are quite impressive pieces; but one has to agree that in order to see such a work, it was necessary to have found a man who loved beautiful things and who had a perfect knowledge of them, such as the one that Monsieur Amelot de Bisceul possesses."

Thus Pierre Cottard, architect of the Hôtel des Ambassadeurs de Hollande, which is also known as Amelot de Bisseuil, judges his work, taken up between 1657 and 1660 in the heart of the Marais district. The painted works described by the architect are none other than those by Poërson, who realized the cupola of the staircase, destroyed in 1760; Simon Vouet, whose ceiling was replaced by a painting by Vien; Boullogne and Jean-Baptiste Corneille, whose works remain partially intact in the Italian-style bedroom and the Gallery of Psyche. In the eighteenth century, the new owner, Louis Tellier, unfortunately undertook some major transformations, including the elimination of the staircase. At this time the town house was rented to Pierre-Augustin Caron de Beaumarchais who operated a weapons business and a goodwill institution out of it . . . which did not prevent him from finishing his most famous play there in 1778, *The Marriage of Figaro*.

Used as a public ballroom during the Revolution, and then as workshops and stores in the nineteenth century, the town house did not recover its luster until 1924. The restorations give an accurate picture of the work realized by Pierre Cottard.

Above: *An exquisite gilded candelabrum is on display in the room of this Paris mansion known as the Salon of Flowers.*

Opposite: *Elegant Louis XV-style furnishings fill the mansion's Salon of Flowers. The painting of a young Greek girl by Jospeh-Marie Vien, which was presented at the French Academy Salon of 1761, is on display above the commode.*

Opposite: *Covered in red silk damask, the furnishings in the Salon of Flowers were made by Delanoy.*

Above: *The Triumph of Flora, as depicted by artist Joseph-Marie Vien, graces the ceiling of the Salon of Flowers.*

Opposite: *A dramatic atmosphere is achieved in the decoration of the mansion's Italian-style sleeping chamber.*

Above: *The stucco curtain, held aloft by putti, creates the impression of an alcove in the Italian-style bedroom.*

Above: *On the ceiling of the bedroom the marriage of Hercules and Hebe, painted by Louis de Boullogne, is celebrated.*

Opposite: *The elaborate stuccowork and gilded surfaces of the bedroom are a tribute to the Grand Siècle.*

Opposite: *Along the walls and on the ceiling of the gallery, Jean-Baptiste Corneille traced the life of Psyche.*

Above: *In this detail of the ceiling, Psyche, said to be too beautiful to marry, is abducted by Eros himself.*

Hôtel Lambert, Paris

If there is a town house in Paris worthy of being called a palace, it is the Hôtel Lambert. Did not Voltaire himself go so far as to say in a letter to the royal prince of Prussia, dated 15 April 1739: "It is a house made for a sovereign who would be a philosopher"? Today that definition has lost none of its significance. The town house was erected by Le Vau in 1632 at the tip of the Ile Saint-Louis for the financier Jean-Baptiste Lambert. With works executed by Charles Le Brun and Eustache Le Sueur, it became a legend at once.

Begun in 1649, the Gallery of Hercules, the first monumental work by Le Brun, served as a point of departure for his work at the Louvre and Versailles. Twenty-three meters long and seven meters wide, the ceiling of this "nave" is divided into five compositions depicting stories of the hero of antiquity. In the nineteenth century, the ceiling was repainted by Delacroix. Le Sueur, sometimes called the "French Raphael," also left eloquent examples of his work: the Room of the Muses (whose five paintings are today found in the Louvre), the Room of the Baths (where Voltaire stayed), and the Room of Love all figure among his masterpieces. At the base of the monumental staircase, modeled on the one at Cluny, the painter has depicted the River and its Naïad; he also decorated the antechamber of the first floor that leads into the Gallery of Hercules with paintings in grisaille. To these exceptional décors, a collection of objects and furniture was gradually added: majolicas, enamels, vases from Saint-Porchaire, furniture by Oeben and Riesner, mounted objects and silver sculptures from Dresden, not to mention the portrait by Ingres or the wall hanging attributed to Rembrandt. So many unique pieces from all ages make up one of the most beautiful and most complete private collections in France.

Above and opposite: *Along the walls of the Hôtel Lambert's main staircase, decorated with motifs inspired by Philibert de l'Orme, hang rich and colorful Beauvais tapestries executed after sketches made by the renowned French painter François Boucher.*

Opposite: *This vestibule leads to the Hercules Gallery and features grisailles attributed to Eustache Le Sueur.*

Above: *In the Hôtel Lambert's Hercules Gallery, bronze reliefs of the labors of Hercules are the work of sculptor Gérard von Opstal.*
Overleaf: *The ceiling in the Hercules Gallery was designed by Le Brun prior to his work at the royal palace of Versailles.*

Above: *The bookshelves that line one wall of the mansion's red salon are fronted by columns of lapis lazuli.*

Opposite: *The two bronze figures atop the bookshelves in the red salon are modeled after sculptures by Michelangelo from the Médicis chapel in Florence. Golden Corinthian capitals top the columns of lapis lazuli on this spectacular piece.*

Opposite: *The more formal air of the eighteenth century pervades the grand salon of the Hôtel Lambert.*

Above: *Objets d'art are arranged on the surface of the lacquered, Riesner-style desk in the grand salon.*

Above: *The Hôtel Lambert partially owes its celebrity to the famous Salon of the Muses, originally decorated by Le Sueur.*

Opposite: *Two polychrome basins, flanking the doorway leading to the mansion's impressive Room of Enamels and Majolicas, are from a set of nine wine coolers commissioned by Guidobaldo, the Duke of Urbino, for his own dining table.*

Opposite: *The Room of Enamels and Majolicas contains treasures that rival those in some of the world's finest museums.*

Above: *This portrait, presumed to be Erasmus, by Jean II Pénicaud, hangs in the Room of Enamels and Majolicas.*

Above: *Vermeil and silver objects of German origin are displayed at the center of the dining-salon table.*

Opposite: *The walls of the dining salon are covered in Flemish leather painted to depict David's entrance into Jerusalem.*

Opposite: *At the end of a suite of rooms hangs the celebrated portrait of Baroness James de Rothschild by Ingres.*

Above: *Venus and Cupid surmount this nineteenth-century Louis XVI-style clock whose pendulum is signed Jacquier.*

Tanlay, Burgundy

Opposite: *Upon a medieval foundation, the château was built on a rectangular plan in the sixteenth century. Left unfinished for almost eighty years, the building was completed by architect Pierre Le Muet during the seventeenth century.*

Tanlay, a half-ruined fortress and unfinished château at the beginning of the seventeenth century, became the palace that we know today between 1643 and 1648: during these five years, the architect Pierre Le Muet (1591–1669) gave free reign to his creativity while embellishing the new home of Italian banker Michel Particelli.

The medieval foundations and Renaissance configuration have been respected, but from that time on, the ensemble took on an even grander bearing. The ornamental alterations of the central façade, the entrance pavilion with its ringed columns and pyramids, the portico closing the perspective with the grand canal, and the stable framing the forecourt give the château a more spectacular dimension and soften the almost military severity of its architecture. Inside, the vestibule of the emperors resting on Doric columns, and the gallery decorated in trompe l'oeil in grisaille (reduced in size after a fire in the eighteenth century) add a classical measure to the décor, the guidelines for which were articulated by Le Muet in 1623 in his *Manière de bien bâtir pour toutes sortes de personnes (A Way of Building for all Kinds of People)*. Following his principles, he rationalizes the layout of the rooms, each one being in proportion with its function.

The treasures of this old fief were preserved by the architect. One of the most remarkable is on the ceiling of the tower, an allegory painting said to be "of the League," referring to the Wars of Religion, a series of civil wars waged in France between 1562 and 1598 by French Protestants.

Opposite: *Obelisks mark the entrance bridge that leads to the gatehouse portal flanked by ringed columns.*

Above: *This wall closes the perspective from the portal, or small château, preceding the main building.*

Opposite: *In the tower, a sixteenth-century ceiling allegorically depicts members of the Médicis court.*

Above: *Janus, the French royal symbol, looks with benevolence at the Catholics and with hostility at the Huguenots.*

Above and opposite: *In the center of the ceiling, the figure of Jupiter observes the scenes of religious tensions.*

Overleaf: *The first-floor gallery of the residence is decorated with grisaille executed by Italian artists.*

Cormatin, Burgundy

Built at the beginning of the seventeenth century by Antoine du Blé d'Uxelles, governor of Chalon, Cormatin has retained the rustic appearance of a family fief. Mistreated over the years, it lost its southern wing at the start of the nineteenth century, but the main body of the house and the building that projects from it at right angles remain, both topped by slate roofs.

The château, still faithful to the architectural principles dictated in the sixteenth century, combines a simplicity of organization and materials with a refinement of certain details: for example, the base of the steep walls, the mullioned windows, and the watchtowers stand in contrast to the entrance portal with its Doric columns surmounted by a bust, and especially the subtlety of its interior décor.

The monumental bare stone staircase, protected by cradle vaults and supported by powerful pillars, marks the floor levels. The carved wood mantlepieces have been preserved; the Cordovan leather panels are enclosed in wainscoting; and the ceilings are painted in the French style. These alterations were undertaken in 1627 by the Marquis d'Uxelles who installed in his new home sixty paintings that had been left to him by his father.

Remarkably restored, Cormatin has recaptured its past splendor and can pride itself on being one of the most original homes in Burgundy today.

Above and opposite: *Richly ornamented ceilings are featured throughout the interior of the grand house.*

Moncley, Franche-Comté

Moncley invites us to examine several stages of the Louis XVI style. The architect Bertrand, a student of Ledoux, began constructing the building in 1778 for the first president of the parliament of Franche-Comté, who later became the Marquis of Terrier-Santans. This is a dwelling without pretensions whose gracefulness is expressed by the curve of its façade, where an Ionic portico surmounted by a pediment has been inscribed, and where the proportions of the salons have remained intact. At the central building, Bertrand joined some sturdy outbuildings whose bossage work Ledoux would not have disclaimed.

Interrupted by the Revolution, construction continued in 1830: at that time, a rotunda was added and the apartments of the left wing took shape. Between 1911 and 1914 there was a revival of the Louis XVI style, and the Count of Lagarde, who took over Moncley at this time, decided to finish the grand vestibule and the chapel accordingly. The château, with its respect for bare white stone and columns, has thus preserved its neoclassical appearance. The interior décor of its salons, displaying a penchant for *rocaille* style, has tempered its noble austerity.

Located between town and country, Moncley, in spite of its alterations, continues to embody the eighteenth-century ideal of a gentleman's house. As proof, the filming of the most recent movie on Fragonard was set at Moncley.

Above and opposite: *The noble vestibule, with its Corinthian columns, is an example of the neoclassical style.*

Overleaf: *To mark the courtyard façade entrance, Bertrand designed the portico supported by Ionic columns.*

Ainay-le-Vieil, Centre

The medieval layout of Ainay-le-Vieil, with its polygonal enclosure and foundation that are approximately one thousand years old, has earned it the nickname that made it famous: the "petit Carcassonne." Situated in the heart of the Cher, between Bourges and Montluçon, this château, with is military appearance and nine watchtowers that were erected in the fourteenth century, was able to reconcile the late Gothic with the early Renaissance. But we must look back to the Middle Ages to find its origins with the family of Guillaume des Barres, who participated in the third crusade in 1191, led by Frederic Barberousse, Philippe Auguste, and Richard the Lion-Hearted.

Ainay-le-Vieil was once the property of Jacques Coeur (1395–1456), a banker and advisor to King Charles VII. Coeur built the famous palace at Bourges that today bears his name. In 1467, it passed into the hands of the Bigny family where it has remained. They made important alterations with the help of regional artists who had already contributed to the improvement of the Jacques Coeur palace and the neighboring château of Meillant. In the new building, a tower staircase rises in a flamboyant style and has been inscribed with the Bigny coat of arms as well as their motto: *Nobilitat virtus exaltatque viros* (Courage ennobles and exalts men). Inside, the monumental polychrome fireplace of the large salon was executed at the beginning of the sixteenth century to commemorate the visit of Louis XII and Anne of Brittany.

Above: *The salon fireplace was built in honor of Louis XII and Anne of Brittany, who once visited the property.*

Opposite: *In the salon, the portrait at left is of Colbert, minister to Louis XIV, an ancestor of the estate's present owners.*

Ansouis, Provence

As far back as 960, Ansouis appeared in French archives as a fortification belonging to the sovereign Forcalquier family. Dominating the Aygue valley, its configuration was quadrilateral with a keep rising from its center; four corner towers were added to this plan during the eleventh and twelfth centuries at the time when the château passed into the hands of the Sabran.

In 1285, this citadel that appears so undisturbed created an unusual legend with the birth of Elzéar de Sabran. The boy, married at the age of thirteen to Delphine de Puy Michel, one of the richest and most chaste heiresses of the region, lived with his virgin wife for thirty years at Ansouis in accordance with the absolute rules of sanctity: the pure couple who vowed their life to God dispensed good deeds and miracles in the region, transforming the fortress into a veritable monastery where the servants had to swear to lead a life as virtuous as that of their masters.

Ansouis, which had remained a solid Catholic bastion until the sixteenth century, fell under the attacks of Huguenot bands. Extensive reconstruction became necessary, and the Renaissance-style structure that we admire today was erected. In the eighteenth century, a large part of its interior was designed, and the gardens and terraces were embellished with a magnificent fifty-meter-long pool. In the feudal section of the château, the bedroom of Delphine and Elzéar (canonized in 1371) has been piously preserved. His cult is still celebrated at Ansouis in the first days of September each year.

Opposite: *Rich velvets and patterned fabrics contribute to the intimate atmosphere of this Ansouis salon.*

Above: *Three painted porcelain Chinese sage figures are an example of the exquisite objects on display at Ansouis.*

Above: *The refined taste of the décor is apparent via the skilled arrangement of objects in this salon.*

Opposite: *Italian wood carvings depicting the four seasons of the year are displayed on the walls of the hall.*

Barbentane, Provence

Between Avignon and Tarascon stands Barbentane. Built of yellow stone from the Gard, it suggests an architectural model of the "Provençale in the Italian style." The design manifests a Tuscan influence mixed with the style of the Grand Siècle, during which time the château was built for Marc-Antoine de Pujet, lord of Barbentane. In 1674, the dwelling was totally transformed by his son, who was a companion in arms of the Great Condé and was immortalized by Madame de Sévigné under the name of "courageous Barbentane." The mannerist impulses of the original building were later abandoned in favor of the classical rigor of the Louis XIV style.

In the eighteenth century, Barbentane underwent its last and most significant alterations. In 1741, a new forepart was attached to the northern façade and the interior was almost completely altered by Thibault, a foreman from Avignon who built the famous "flat vaults" (1750), whose stereotomy can be admired in the series of adjoining salons.

The restrained and joyful sumptuousness of Italy left its mark on Barbentane some decades later, when Joseph de Pujet returned from his post as French ambassador in Florence, which he held from 1768 to 1788. The marbles from Carrara and Venice, the hard stones, and the consoles were incorporated into a décor that still included Louis XV furniture, astounding rococo wood carvings, and bathrooms (or "little houses" as they were called) decorated with plaster of Paris. Enhanced by outbuildings and terraced gardens, Barbentane found its permanent identity at last.

Above: *A lion statue is displayed on an Italian marble console, one of the many fine pieces in the château's collection.*

Opposite: *The main staircase at Barbentane features an elaborately detailed eighteenth-century ironwork railing.*

Opposite: *A rare rococo-style salon features a Venetian fireplace.* Above: *Detail, salon fireplace mantel.*

Above: *Alternating stripes of green and white marble cover the floor in the Château de Barbentane's statuary salon.*

Opposite: *The boldly patterned floor in the dining salon is made of marble imported from Carrara, Italy.*

Opposite: *The decoration of the grand salon is in keeping with the style associated with eighteenth-century Provence.*

Above: *Built into the corner of this sleeping chamber is a* "petite maison" *designed to enclose a bathroom.*

Roquetaillade, Aquitaine

Opposite and overleaf: *A fourteenth-century fortress, Roquetaillade is one of the most pleasing of Viollet-le-Duc's restorations.*

Could there be a prouder and at the same time odder fortress in France than Roquetaillade? An unparalleled example of medieval militarism that was revised in the nineteenth century, this heroic "bastille," built in 1306, dominates the valley between Langon and Bazas. It stands on a cliff and its walls with six round crenelated towers form a rectangle; in the center, a square keep rising up thirty-five meters has withstood all attacks.

Commissioned by the Cardinal Gaillard de la Mothe, nephew of Pope Clement V, Roquetaillade came into the possession of the Marquis and Marquise de Mauvesin in the middle of the nineteenth century. Philippe Jullian writes that they turned to Viollet-le-Duc, "the busiest architect in France, to give their château the brilliance it never had." The work began in 1860 and did not end until 1875 with the completion of the chapel; its décor, for the most part conceived by Duthuit, a brilliant student of Viollet-le-Duc, included an abundance of mosaics, enamels, gildings, and polychrome ceilings.

In spite of the alterations, the severity of the building has been respected: the drawbridge, crenelations, and glass windows were simply added to the original structure. Inside, every bed had a canopy, every bedroom a monumental fireplace, and every staircase a gilded bronze oil lamp. Colorful and floral motifs, heraldic symbols, and the depiction of fantastical animals made the interiors at once grandiose and cozy. Is it a setting for an opera of the Second Empire or for a Gothic cathedral? Above all, Roquetaillade is the home of a prince, where Walter Scott would have loved to dream up crusades.

Opposite: *A rather simple stone chapel, completed in 1875, was built on the grounds of the château.*

Above: *Viollet-le-Duc designed the rather flamboyant polychrome interior scheme for the chapel at Roquetaillade.*

Above: *Columns crowned with delicate leaves support the regal stairway, decorated with coats of arms.*

Opposite: *A Renaissance fireplace was preserved during the renovation of a salon now used as a meeting room.*

Opposite: *The nineteenth-century interpretation of the medieval style is apparent in the decoration of a bedroom.*

Above: *A rustic beamed ceiling hangs above the comfortably furnished salon used as a reading room.*

Above: *The principal rooms, such as this dining salon, have remained much as Viollet-le-Duc designed them.*

Opposite: *The exuberance of nineteenth-century decorative style pervades this sleeping chamber at Roquetaillade.*

Château-Lafite, Aquitaine

Opposite: *Restored during the seventeenth and eighteenth centuries, the château was built in the late Middle Ages.*

One cannot speak of Château-Lafite without mentioning the wine produced there, a veritable fountain of youth, "comparable to the ambrosia of the gods on Olympus," according to the Marshal de Richelieu. Quickly adopted by Louis XV and his court, this "divine nectar" was classified as the first of the *grands crus* of Médoc in 1855. The wine's grapes take root in the blessed soil of Aquitaine, in the heart of the property surrounding the château, which was begun in the fifteenth century and subsequently greatly altered.

Each age has left to the property its testimony: the Renaissance a watch tower, the seventeenth century a staircase, the eighteenth wood carvings and plaster moldings in the bedrooms. But it is to the sumptuous Second Empire décor conceived by the new owner in 1868 that we should turn our attention. Because if among the successive owners of Château-Lafite one should be remembered, it should surely be the Baron James de Rothschild. In acquiring this new home for 4,410,000 francs in gold, the famous banker marked a stage in the history of taste. He immediately gave the place its identity by altering the salons with comfortable upholstered furniture in red, green, and yellow; carpets with floral designs; and damasks embroidered with braids that cover the walls. Ingres painted his wife's portrait; Honoré de Balzac, composer Giacomo Meyerbeer, and poet Heinrich Heine were visitors to the Rothschilds' private hôtel in Paris.

Thus more than anywhere else, the land of the divine bottle, the taste of art, and the art of taste were linked to Lafite.

Above: *Rich green damask and velvet fabrics cover the chairs, walls, and windows of the château's library.*

Opposite: *The spirit of the Second Empire is kept alive in the decoration of the salon at Château-Lafite.*

Vayres, Aquitaine

On the outskirts of Dordogne, resembling a palace or ghostly citadel, Vayres—an old holding of the kings of England, who were dukes and masters of Aquitaine in the eighteenth century—dominates a butte ten kilometers from Libourne. Though its origins go back to the eleventh century, today it is for the most part a Renaissance and seventeenth-century château that stands before us. Given to Cesar Borgia as part of his young bride's dowry in 1499, the château already had some of the features we see today. A large tower, visible from the court, was attached to a wing that had been skillfully altered and animated by bay windows, arcades, and niches in the Renaissance style. The work was executed by the engineer and architect Louis de Foix for the new owner of Vayres, Ogier de Gourgue, governor of finances in Bordeaux and counselor of state. Vayres was previously owned by Henry of Navarre, the future King Henry IV.

The Italian-style façade opens on the gardens, which are now decorated by flower beds in the French style that were created in the twentieth century. The façade took on its definitive shape in 1695, having suffered badly during the Fronde: at this time the central pavilion, crowned by a dome and skylight, was extended to include a suite of staircases linked with a series of double banisters weaving a geometric pattern between building and landscape. The classical character of this unique, crenelated building is augmented by pilasters and a pediment that decorate the pavilion, as well as by a peristyle with ringed columns alternately vermiculated.

Acknowledgments

Our thanks go first to all the property owners who willingly opened their doors to us and showed us such patience and kindness. In particular, we wish to thank Valentine de Ganay, without whom this book would not have been possible, as well as the Baroness Elie de Rothschild, Jean and Thierry Feray, Jean-Louis Gaillemin, Elisabeth Lebovici, Shirley Johnston, and Madame Kolesnikoff.

L.M. & R.S.